THE ART OF FLOW

40 Reflections on Being Fully Present

Yolanda Lidia Valdés, Ph.D.

Copyright © 2022 by Yolanda Lidia Valdés, Ph.D.

YolandaValdes.com

All rights reserved. No part of this publication may be reproduced, distributed, or transmitted in any form or by any means, including photocopying, recording, or other electronic or mechanical methods, without the prior written permission of the publisher, except in the case of brief quotations embodied in critical reviews and certain other non-commercial uses permitted by copyright law.

For permission requests, write to the author at: hello@zentaohome.com

The Art of Flow / Yolanda Lidia Valdés, Ph.D. —1st ed.

ISBN Hardcover 978-1-7365698-3-2
ISBN Paperback 978-1-7365698-2-5

DEDICATION

This book is dedicated in gratitude to nature,
my greatest teacher.

In memory of my father, who devoted his life to serving others
in presence and happiness.

To my dearest friends Ernesto Carazza for his inspiration and clarity.
Macarena Luz Bianchi for her unconditional support.

To all students and seekers and wanderers of life.

CONTENTS

1. Flow 8
2. Inner Teacher 10
3. Faith 12
4. Meeting Love 14
5. Summer Cleanse 16
6. Finding Clarity 18
7. Witness 20
8. Surrender 22
9. Enlighten Yourself 24
10. Embrace 26
11. Sensing 28
12. Grace 30
13. Remove Fully 32
14. Acceptance 34
15. Truth Is Love 36
16. The Body 38
17. The Spirit 40
18. Comfort 42
19. Pathways 44
20. Synchronicity 46

21. Nature 48
22. Changing Wind 50
23. The Heavens 52
24. Hope 54
25. Eternity 56
26. Resonance 58
27. Holiness 60
28. Gentleness 62
29. Compassion 64
30. Belonging 66
31. Presence 68
32. Opportunity 70
33. Creation 72
34. Present Moment 74
35. Beyond Conditioning . . . 76
36. Emotional Compass 78
37. Authenticity 80
38. Balance 82
39. Perfectly Imperfect 84
40. Gentle Manner 86

This collection of forty short reflections invites you on a journey toward a deeper state of flow. Written during the solitude of the pandemic and overcoming a dark night of the soul, I share my observations of nature, love, and presence. Each reflection provides an opportunity for contemplation and the possibility to further harmony with the now.

May the flow be with you now and always!

1
FLOW

The vessel cannot be filled, as it is already One with All. We are complete and perfect, but we unknowingly act from a state of lack. We are filled with the light and love of the Universe, but we fail to see things as they are. To be in the Flow is to witness all thoughts, emotions, and events with an open heart. To flow with life is to flow as life—thus remembering who you are.

2
INNER TEACHER

Listen to your inner teacher.

It will gently and effortlessly move
you through life.

You are never the one who is moving alone.

You are always taken care of.

This is unchangeable.

What changes over the course of your life is the
veil of illusion, which slowly melts away.

3
FAITH

Surrender to faith and commit to living your life in gratitude.

Then you will gain access to its true magic.

No matter how hard things get in life, we must find comfort in Faith. Faith is the foundation of any size accomplishment. We need faith to succeed, to find the resources to accomplish the goal. And if we find obstacles along the way, faith becomes the driving force to find ways and solutions to move forward. At that very moment, we have the option to sit quietly in prayer, seeking strength from deep inside. When we become aware of God's Nature, which is returning to your inner balance, it immediately replaces all fears.

4
MEETING LOVE

Meeting love can move your emotions freely in an unrecognized direction, a joyous exploration into parts of you that your lover's light brings out, connected to an inner explosion of sensory fullness.

5

SUMMER CLEANSE

Get out, expand yourself!

The waves of the ocean are waiting for you to wash your face, to cleanse your soul of the wounds you have endured and stored in the chamber of your personal history.

6
FINDING CLARITY

Dive deeply into your heart. Rest there for a while. Listen to the answer your soul wants to give you. Do not rush to receive the response, for you may be disappointed or have an internal quarrel with yourself.

Rest and move as you receive the strength needed. You will know as it grows in you as a radiant light giving you wings to take you where you are meant to be.

7
WITNESS

Transparent, translucent, obscured—it's how we can see each other through the lens of our beliefs.

8
SURRENDER

The more you hold on to a person, place, or thing, the more it will eventually turn on you.

Hold space, let go, and allow the freedom of what does not ask to be held.

9
ENLIGHTEN YOURSELF

Raise your eyes. Connect deeply with Him who is One with what is not lost.

10
EMBRACE

Sit and embrace your body, quietness, words, playfulness, this beautiful story and all its raw edges.

11
SENSING

What is your heart telling you about your surroundings?

If it is more change, welcome it and let it flow. Feel deep within and let it consume you in the heart's fire. This is being in it without controlling any outcome. What feels good to your heart—to your body—is an invitation to explore.

12
GRACE

Oh, Universe, you that are so
ever present in our lives, help us become
aware of your grace.

13

REMOVE FULLY

Life removes from our lives everything that does not belong. We try to hold on to that which is hurtful, thinking that we deserve it. The inner voice quietly advises that it does not belong, but we are comfortable with the hurt because letting go is letting go of a part of us that is deeply stocked to our core for survival, for a story. We fight it and justify it, but our higher self has a plan we do not see. When we hold on to that which no longer serves us, our higher self comes in and removes it. It is painful to let go of what no longer serves us. It will not help us evolve into the fruition of our mission. When removed, it comes upon us as loneliness—the nakedness leaving us wanting to fulfill the empty hole.

14
ACCEPTANCE

No past, no future.

There is only this instant if you are willing to see things in a new way.

15

TRUTH IS LOVE

There is only the infinite and eternal extension of love.

We are part of this conscious, loving process of Creation.

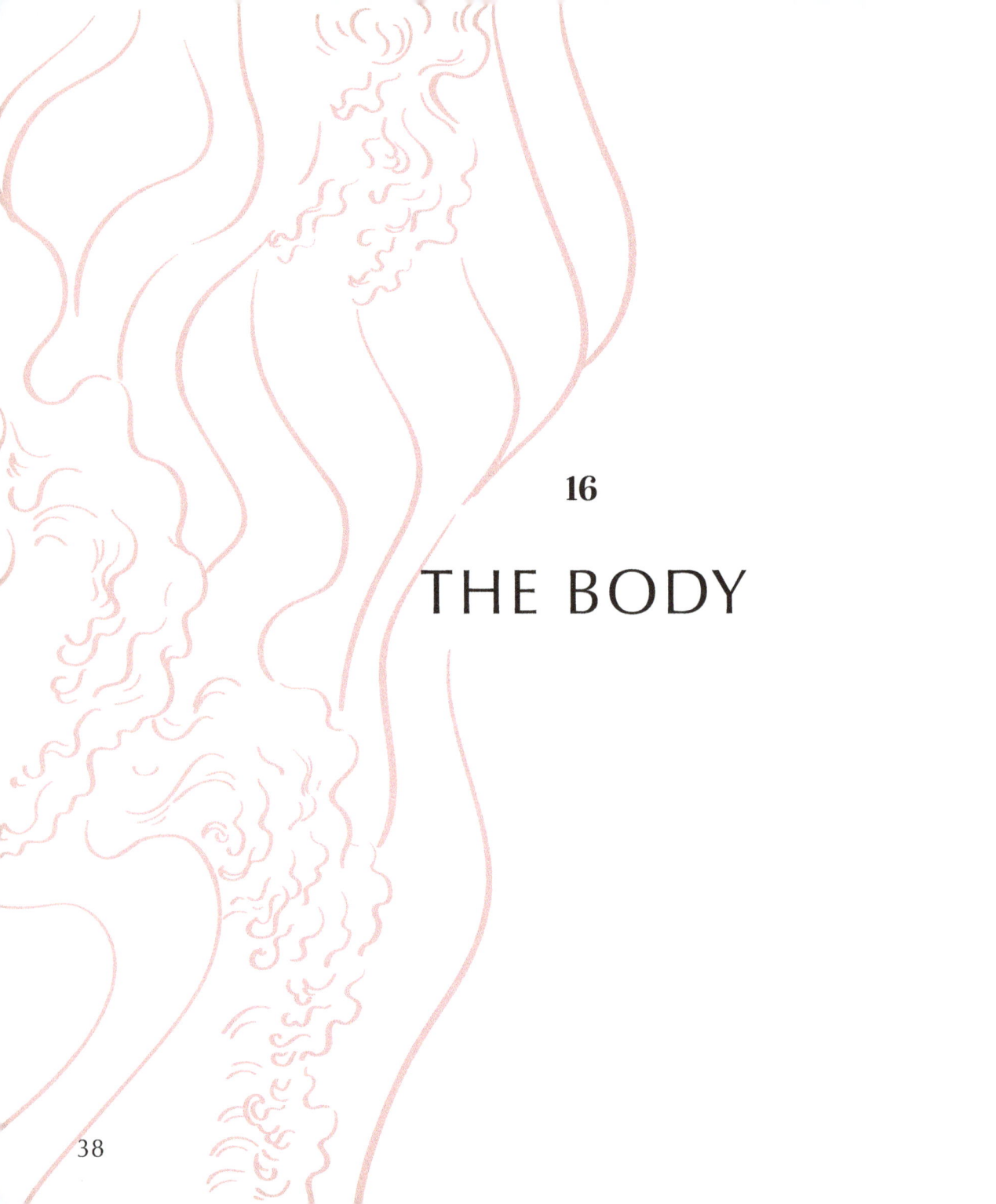

16
THE BODY

The body is an instrument. It's up to us the purpose for which it is used.

It can be used to communicate or separate, for healing or to hurt, for peace or conflict, for love or fear.

Within us, there is the Wisdom to make this choice.

17
THE SPIRIT

The Spirit speaks through us even through the deep abyss of our experiences.

Trust it!

18
COMFORT

To find comfort does not necessarily mean to relax. It is like doing anything that makes you feel cushioned up, cradled in the abyss of life. What are you risking when you are in comfort? Is this looking to be embraced by the environment in which you live? Looking for comfort is more than finding a place, a pair of shoes, a house, or a secret place. Comfort is surrender to that which struggles less. The cushion of life lets you make choices that have been to your comfort. Our hearts long to feel caressed by the beating breath of our higher self, which is always present in our lives. Dwelling in comfort is being aligned with our higher self, which provides all the abundance available in awareness. Soothing the suffering is finding a way out of that which we refuse to look at.

19
PATHWAYS

Pathways are shaped through our journey to discover our depths—to become liberated.

20
SYNCHRONICITY

Signs, symbols, and messages are how the Universe speaks to us, confirming if we are on the right or wrong path manifesting in this journey that we call life.

You can learn to discern what is revealed to you for your highest good and for all those involved.

21
NATURE

Nature speaks to us uninterruptedly of developments, growth, and maturation.

What appears like a cycle of birth and death is indeed a reflection of the process of Life always expanding Itself.

There is no reason to try to oppose this process and limit it because of our fear of change and our lack of trust in life.

There is no true life without the search for ourselves, for our deep transcendent face, without giving up our false identifications.

22
CHANGING WIND

The experience of standing in front of a stormy ocean with the wind ripping the tops off the waves can be very humbling. It all helps keep one's perspective on how many things in this world are insignificant compared to the forces of nature.

When wind moves without warning to create change with unknown strength, taking everything that is not sturdy, it reminds me of challenging and changing times.

We cannot oppose our true purpose in life. We can only learn to follow the path that Love has prepared for us.

23

THE HEAVENS

The tree leaves have veins facing upward, reaching in awareness to the heavens for nourishment in the early sunrise.

24
HOPE

Is it water or something more as I glance at the rain?

Rainfall is a blessing to a dry land in which thirsty creatures long for water, bringing them hope and life.

25

ETERNITY

Eternity looks for no past nor future.

In time, the only way
to access eternity is this instant.

26
RESONANCE

The tone of your voice can carry either hostility or peace.

What is yours saying?

27

HOLINESS

Holiness is the real condition of Being, the source of awareness, and the profound realization of the "I am."

In holiness, as you grow, everything grows.

You are not separated from holiness, like a bird's feather is not separated from the flying process.

Within and beyond, you are holy and precious. Holiness overflows everywhere, and you can become an ongoing source and manifestation of it.

28
GENTLENESS

Gentleness represents a warm and compassionate approach toward yourself and the world. It is treating yourself with the utmost care and establishing an intimate relationship with the parts of yourself that you have neglected. The foundation of gentleness is self-love; also, the practice of being gentle reveals your extraordinary potential for love.

29

COMPASSION

Compassion represents divine connection.

Compassion opens the heart and anchors you in the present moment. It attunes you to the vastness and holiness of all things. When you are compassionate, you are mindfully walking your path without interference from the ego-directed mind.

When you are out of compassion, you are not only out of alignment but also out of yourself. Compassion blooms whenever you are present. It unlocks your eternal self and welcomes you in togetherness. Through compassion, you become one with the parts of yourself that you rejected, and, most importantly, you become one with the universe. And you begin to understand where the misunderstanding, anger, and confusion come from.

30
BELONGING

Belonging opens the door of inner freedom, gives hope, and builds confidence.

31
PRESENCE

Presence is effortless and spontaneous, abundant, and containing nothing. It represents the ultimate and universal condition—innate expression. We cease to do anything, only to realize the gracefulness of all that has been done through us, by us, for us. As you become present, you experience a state of ecstatic completion. In presence, you are lovingly welcomed back home into pure blissfulness and conscious beingness. Here and Now, you understand that you are the one you were always waiting for.

32
OPPORTUNITY

Opportunity lies in thought.

We sometimes forget the most crucial aspect of existence on this Earth: the endless stream of co-creative energy that flows through us all. The Universe's abundance is limitless: there is absolutely no outer obstacle that could keep you away from designing your world. The limits we perceive are born in the unconscious mind; once cleared and integrated, we gain access to opportunity.

To fully use our creative capacity, we need to understand opportunity from a sacred point of view. Once dedicated to our higher purpose, the doors of perception cleanse themselves, and we can allow spiritual power to flow in our lives. Opportunity is the by-product of our higher mind; it represents our inner openness toward intention.

33
CREATION

Aligning evermore with the purpose of Creation, we witness the beautiful synchronicities that bring meaning to everyday living.

True intention anchors us in a higher state of perception and recognition.

The more we aim toward what we really want, the better we manifest on all levels.

34
PRESENT MOMENT

Non-duality represents the essence and truth of all that is, beyond this world's illusions. It is ungraspable and uncontainable, yet ever flowing with Presence. Non-duality is a state of wholeness—the ultimate completion of Being beyond all the illusions of separation from every living thing. It is the condition of Eternity, reflected in the Now, as this is the only moment that exists in time.

Being in the present moment is simple, and simplicity is the language of Spirit. Awareness cannot be forced on someone. Yet you can practice putting all your awareness in the present moment. There is no need for restoration, as nothing is broken or missing within you. Just be and see what happens. Witness the "doer" and the "thinker" soften into the "I am." A limited personal perspective contracts you, but the infinite Universal perspective expands you. Allow to rise and go within at the same time. Acknowledge this is your true endless nature. And you can merge into the ocean of awareness in the Now.

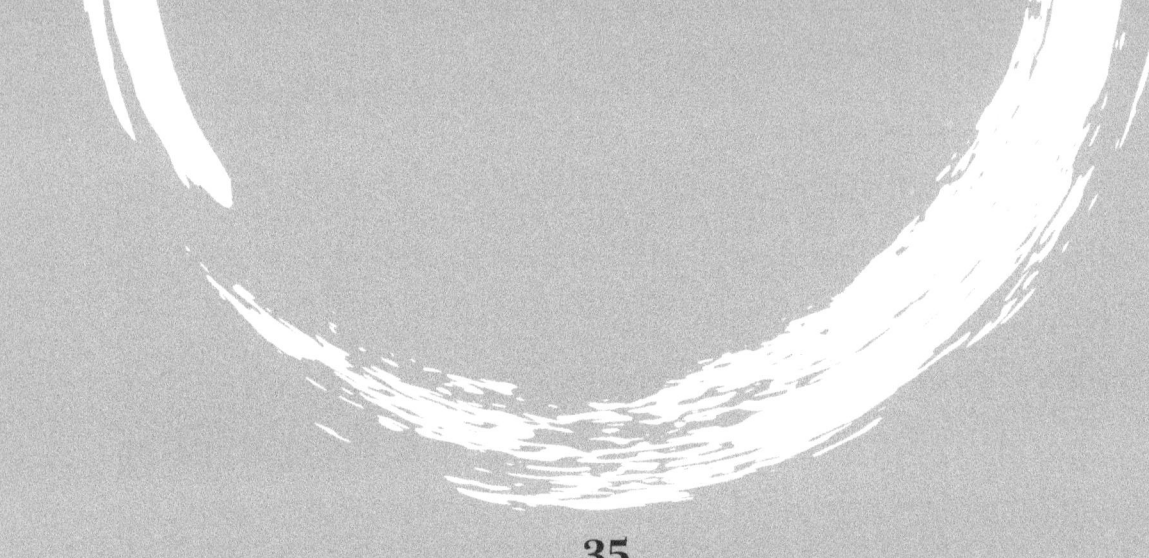

35

BEYOND CONDITIONING

Living our truth entails disengaging from the patterns and filters that alter how we see ourselves and our environment.

36
EMOTIONAL COMPASS

Your emotions reveal to you your deep attitude toward everything in the world.

37
AUTHENTICITY

Authenticity—the courage and deep desire to be yourself. It is rooted in accepting all levels of the self and the impermanence of one's life story. Practicing authenticity represents the ability to respond with grace and honesty to whatever arises. One can be authentic only within a state of presence and self-acceptance. Being authentic is not an ego-directed tendency toward perfectionism, but it has everything to do with changing one's perspective on life from a separative point of view to an all-including one. Authenticity embodies humility and a deep sense of understanding and embracing the growth path that we walk during our lives.

38

BALANCE

Balance holds the key to a deeper understanding of everything: an experience that exceeds any perceived barriers and launches us directly into the heart dimension.

39

PERFECTLY IMPERFECT

You are not broken, and you never were.

As you begin to see and forgive your faults, you learn how to see yourself deeply.

Seeing yourself truly goes hand in hand with recognizing the truth in others.

40
GENTLE MANNER

Treating yourself gently pulls you out from an effortful survival mode and encourages you to abide in relaxation and easiness; it softens the edges of perception and inspires you to commit to a life of loving-kindness.

THANK YOU, TRUTH SEEKER!

I appreciate you taking this journey of self reflection with me. I trust it was exactly how your soul wanted to grow. May it continue to enrich you.

I love to hear from my readers, please follow me on Instagram @yoli.valdes and visit my website at YolandaValdes.com to join my email list for exclusive content.

If you enjoyed this book, a simple way to support me is to leave a positive review and share about it with your family and friends.

May the flow be with you now and always!

You are not broken, and you never were.

As you begin to see and forgive your faults, you learn how to see yourself deeply.

Seeing yourself truly goes hand in hand with recognizing the truth in others.

40
GENTLE MANNER

Treating yourself gently pulls you out from an effortful survival mode and encourages you to abide in relaxation and easiness; it softens the edges of perception and inspires you to commit to a life of loving-kindness.

THANK YOU, TRUTH SEEKER!

I appreciate you taking this journey of self reflection with me. I trust it was exactly how your soul wanted to grow. May it continue to enrich you.

I love to hear from my readers, please follow me on Instagram @yoli.valdes and visit my website at YolandaValdes.com to join my email list for exclusive content.

If you enjoyed this book, a simple way to support me is to leave a positive review and share about it with your family and friends.

May the flow be with you now and always!

ABOUT THE AUTHOR

Yolanda Lidia Valdés, Ph.D., is an intuitive healer, holistic life counselor, and spiritual director; creator of ZENTAO, whose methodologies are rooted in Eastern philosophies.

Her mission is to empower, support, and educate women to find lasting wholeness by guiding them to restore and embrace their feminine virtues for personal growth, transformation, and self-healing and invite greater flow into their lives.

YolandaValdes.com

www.ingramcontent.com/pod-product-compliance
Lightning Source LLC
Chambersburg PA
CBHW051332110526
44590CB00032B/4488